Odes & Rhymes

Of Life & Times

Book 2

The Funnier Side of Life

By

AJ Brewster

☻

Also by AJ Brewster

Odes & Rhymes of Life & Times Book 1 ~ Alternative Advice on the Adult Adventure (2012)

By Any Other Name (2012)

4

☺

☺

This book is dedicated to all my friends and family who have stood by me over the years with my writing and my website, www.thetwistedtalesofajbrewster.com. Especially to my Granddad Jim, for without him I wouldn't have this crazy sense of humour.

Here is one to get you started.

Poetry is not Boring

Poetry doesn't have to be boring,
It's not always about heartache & love,
You do find there's a lot that is slushy,
But a good poet can write other stuff.

Poetry should be written from the heart,
About things you see and do every day,
About issues you feel really strongly about,
And funny things that make you giggle away.

This book is mostly poems of humour,
With a few on the serious side,
But it's all about things seen through my eyes,
So enjoy the Odes & Rhymes ride.

☺

Contents

Section 1 – Oh Do Behave!

Section 2 - My Life's Little Pleasures

☺

Section 3 – The World's Gone Mad

Section 4 – Horrifying Rhymes

Section 5 – Shits & Giggles

Section 6 – On a More Serious Note

☺

☺

Oh Do Behave!

☺

Duvet Deadlock

The alarm rings out but I cannot seem to rise,

The duvet has me trapped it's a force field in disguise,

Enveloped in its comfort it tricks me into thinking,

That I can waste the day in bed and spend it forty-winking.

The alarm rings out again and I manage to free one arm,

With a quick smack of my hand I hit snooze on the alarm,

Like a hypnotist the Duvet convinces me that it's best,

To lay there snuggled up despite my feeble protest.

The alarm rings out again but I'm trying to ignore,

It's constant shrilling ring because I'd just as soon as snore,

I'd like to tell work I'm ill and ignore the bloody clock,

But I cannot ring in sick with a case of Duvet Deadlock.

What *not* to do While in Your Own World

While waiting for the lights,

I see you sitting in your car,

Oblivious to what's around you,

Your mind is way off far,

Unaware of who is watching,

Your car becomes your shell,

But as your finger disappears up your nose,

It makes me want to yell....

Do bogies have calories?

Do they make you fat?

While you sit there chewing on your greens,

Are you considering that?

Do bogies have calories?

Are they one of your five a day?

And if you pick your nose will your brains fall out,

Like mother used to say?

When you're feeling a little hungry,

And you're stuck in a traffic queue,

Your lunch box empty,

And you've nothing else to chew,

You think that no one sees you,

As your finger goes up your snout,

To root around for a quick meal,

It makes me want to shout.....

Do bogies have calories?

Do they make you fat?

While you sit there chewing on your greens,

Are you considering that?

Do bogies have calories?

Are they one of your five a day?

And if you pick your nose will your brains fall out,

Like mother used to say?

Everyone has an Alter Ego except for Me

Superman has Clark Kent,

Batman has Bruce Wayne,

I tried to find my super powers,

But it all just seemed in vain.

The only web that I could spin,

Seemed to come out of my nose,

I could be just like the Beast because,

I have super hairy toes.

Super heroes have an outfit,

Maybe that's what I was lacking?

So I donned a spandex onesie,

Then taking it off I done my back in.

I tried walking through walls,

I tried moving things with my mind,

I ended up with headaches,

Even more so when combined.

If I have a special power,

I still don't know what it could be,

It seems everyone has an alter ego,

Except,

For,

Me.

Star Wars the Movie Soap Opera

If Star Wars wasn't set in a galaxy far, far away,

But instead was set somewhere on Earth in present day,

Do you think it would have been quite so interesting?

Would we be so riveted by the plot of incest and lies?

And would the big reveal still make us gasp with surprise?

And would it taken have Coronation Street to the cleaners in the soap awards?

If it was Dirt Bikes not Speed Bikes would the chase be so exciting?

And with no such thing as a Lightsaber to use when they were fighting,

How would the son prevent himself from being forced into the family business?

Would the Rebels be wearing hoodies while the Empire dressed in suits?

And would they take to the streets to fight out differences and disputes?

And would Chewbacca be likened to a hairy long distance lorry driver that enjoyed chewing tobacco?

Transfer Window Blues

All the players we know and love get pushed onto the bench,

Or get loaned out to other teams it really makes no sense.

I can understand the sales, though the prices are obscene,

It's hard to see key players go coz fans grow to love *the* team.

A good manager should realise that a squad is like an alliance,

Team's players need time to gel it's hardly rocket science.

But how can they work together when key players are sent away?

Just days before the season starts with no time to practice play.

The club spends loads of money to get the next big player,

But if they don't fit within the team then we really don't have a prayer.

Then the club moves down the table with every game we lose,

And that's why I end up suffering the Transfer Window Blues.

I Blame You Barbara Cartland

I blame you Barbara Cartland,

For following my heart and not my brain,

For encouraging me to believe in romance,

And not advising me of the pain.

I blame you Barbara Cartland,

Your books are just full of lies,

They make me feel like I have a chance,

And then somebody makes me cry.

I blame you Barbara Cartland,

You're as bad as a Disney Cartoon,

Promising 'happily ever after's,

With courteous men who make me swoon.

I blame you Barbara Cartland,

You promised me that I'd have my prince,

But the men can't seem to dress themselves,

And visible pants just make me wince.

I blame you Barbara Cartland,

For not writing a helpful thing,

From now on I'm going to avoid your books,

And just stick with Stephen King.

Mind Your Ps & Qs

A 'please' would be nice when you're asking for a favour,

Good manners aren't something you should deliberately waiver,

And a 'thank you' once the job is done just wouldn't go amiss,

Because a life without manners can never be bliss.

There's really no need to live your life being rude,

Because your day is going wrong and you're in a bad mood,

Don't take it out on others, remember to be polite,

Or your day could go from bad to worse by the start of the night.

If you forget to use your P's and Q's I'll be deaf to your request,

And if you want something done don't put this to the test,

I'm pretty sure you were brought up not dragged up as they say,

So mind your P's and Q's if you want me along to play.

Thank you

MISSING! One Sock

In this crazy world we live in,

Renowned for being strange,

The weirdest things can happen,

Which no one can explain.

For example that missing sock,

That once made up a pair,

Where does really go to?

What does it do when there?

Is my washing machine a wormhole,

To a different time in space?

And when my missing sock gets there,

Will it be clean or a dirty disgrace?

I'd imagine it leaves on the spin cycle,

Vanishing through a black and white funnel,

Lost in a swirling maze of past,

Like they do on that Sixties show *Time Tunnel.*

Or does it end up in a world,

Of lonely missing socks?

Just looking for its sock soul mate,

Under every single rock.

Maybe there should be a dating site,

Where single socks could meet,

A matching sock that's longing for,

A chance to cover feet.

Holiday sickness

I'm harbouring a little germ,

But it's not quite ready to show,

Next week I go on holiday,

Tell me how does that little germ know?

It hangs on with all of its might,

Waiting for my holiday to start,

Gestating and germinating,

Until work day and I do part.

As soon as I clock off for my leave,

The sniffles begin to show,

And as I drive home in my car I feel,

The fever sweats on my brow.

Then all my plans are cancelled,

As, once home, I feel half dead,

And if it's Christmas you can guarantee,

Bam! Christmas will be spent in bed.

So I spend all of my holiday,

Laid up and feeling weak,

Moaning, groaning and rolling around,

While my outlook seems pretty bleak.

But the minute my holiday is over,

The sickness is magically gone,

It seems, just in time to go back to work,

I have the energy to go carry on.

Devil's DIY

I hate the dreaded wallpaper,

I can never get it straight,

And when it comes to DIY,

I'm not anyone's 'Workmate'.

I find DIY a challenge,

That I start but never get done,

And it can never be 'Hammer Time',

Because I always hit my thumb.

I'm a demon with a roller,

But that's nothing to shout about,

I get more paint in my hair,

And my 'cutting in' is just so 'out'.

DIY is just a devil,

Something I would rather 'Gloss' over,

So I'll let you do it for me,

While I watch you from my sofa.

☺

☺

My Life's Little Pleasures

☺

Me and My Yellow Car

People often ask me why I bought a yellow car,

I tell them that it's cheery and it takes me pretty far.

They often say I'm crazy keeping it clean must drive me mad,

But I love to wash my car and that doesn't make me sad.

'C'mon', they ask, 'What's the real reason, please tell us the truth?'

And then I say 'Did you notice the panoramic roof?'

But the real reason I bought it is because of my evil streak,

Knowing while I drive it round of the havoc it will wreak.

I drive past kids in playgrounds sometimes I go by twice,

Or driving past a school at lunch can be kind of nice.

Laughing as I pass the kids inflicting pain to maim,

Giving each other dead arms as they play the Yellow Car Game.

Remote Access

I wish they'd never invented the bloody TV remote,

It drives me to distraction because it's taken away my vote,

I can't watch what I want to and I am willing to negotiate,

He always flicks past my favourite show without even a debate,

The only time I get control is when my partner's gone,

And flicked through every channel and decided there's nothing on.

My Brother & I

My brother and I,

As thick as thieves,

Running round the garden,

Playing Indian Chiefs,

Climbing trees,

Making dens,

Just hanging around,

Like real good friends.

But when we got home,

It was a different matter,

The peace of play,

Was completely shattered,

Doors would slam,

And tables would fly,

As the arguing began,

Between my brother and I.

My brother and I,

Fought like dog and cat,

Growing up was hard,

But enough about that,

We're the best of friends now,

Like macaroni & cheese,

But we still find the time,

For a quick sibling tease.

All It Takes Is Just a Smile

It doesn't take a that much,

Just to add a special touch,

And go that extra mile,

All it takes is just a smile,

Like the gentleman on my street,

Who is really kind of sweet,

I do not know his name,

But every day is just the same,

As I drive past in the morning,

All grumpy and still yawning,

He waves and smiles my way,

And makes me happy for the day.

Granddad Groaners

Oh how I love my Granddad,

His humour and his jokes,

Especially the one-liners,

Told only by old blokes.

I call them Granddad Groaners,

These jokes will never grow old,

You've heard them many times before,

And can't help but laugh when told.

Collected over the years,

From comedians old and young,

The joke starts out quite well,

But by the end you've guessed the pun.

I really love my Granddad,

Because he makes me laugh a lot,

By telling me Granddad Groaners like,

"When a small onion runs out, that's shallot".

Money Tree

I bought myself a money tree but it's yet to grow a note,

Not even a single penny despite how much I hope,

I water it every single day on it I really dote,

I hope it flowers soon because I need a winter coat.

I bought myself a money tree and called it Maxamillion,

I'm hoping with a name like that it will deliver me a trillion,

But when it comes to money I would settle for a billion,

But if I had that money would it make me a better civilian?

Sorry, I Nearly Forgot

I just can't seem to remember,

What I've forgotten to do I forget,

But I know I've forgotten to do something,

And I'll remember too late you can bet.

I hope it wasn't something important,

Or even worse something urgent to do,

My brain cells are still ticking over,

Did I forget to do something for you?

Did I forget to water the plants?

Or did I forget to feed my pets?

Did I forget to lock the front door?

Or a crucial appointment at the vets?

There's something I have forgotten,

And it's driving me insane,

What the hell is wrong with my memory bank?

I only seem to remember the inane.

I forget everything that's important,

But can remember what happened years ago,

Like fainting in the playground at Primary,

While playing in the 1980's winter snow.

I can wow friends with my amazing memory,

Of times we went out and had fun,

But when it came to writing this poem,

I nearly forgot that it wasn't done.

I Am Who I Am

This is me,

I am who I am,

You might not like it,

But I couldn't give a damn.

I'm not here to please you,

I am here to be me,

I'm not a conformist,

This is the way I want to be.

I don't follow the rules,

I follow my own,

I believe what I want to believe,

Not what I'm shown.

I am an individual,

I am not one of your herd,

I have a mind of my own,

And a voice to be heard.

I am not *The Prisoner*,

And this is not Orwell's '84,

If I cannot have my views,

You can leave by that door.

I won't follow your fashion,

I will wear what I like,

And expensive designers,

You can all take a hike.

If I don't like your music,

Then I will not tune in,

To the DJ who's play list,

Is only fit for the bin.

Of course this is my opinion,

And you don't have to hear it,

But I am who I am,

So you'd better get used to it.

Ode to My Best Friend

When I'm in the thick of it,

Knee high in the shit of it,

You've always been there for me.

I've returned the favour when I could,

I guess you knew I always would,

Because we're the best of friends you see.

It might be months between talking to one another,

We might not always see each other,

But we know we're always there.

We've got through some sad times together,

Seen each other through stormy weather,

Because we're best friends and we care.

I got you through your first horror movie,

You're still not so keen and that's groovy,

We'll watch a comedy instead.

We're the best of friends through thick and thin,

And no matter what pickle we're in,

One of us will keep our head.

Despite the fact we're growing older,

We know there'll always be a shoulder,

And a hug to see us through.

I'll never ever feel distressed,

Because I know that I am blessed,

To have a best friend in you.

Soaking Away in the Bath

Soaking away in the bath,

Laying there reading my book,

Glass of wine on the side,

Water so hot I could cook.

Bubbles to promote relaxation,

Candles release my favourite smell,

Soaking away in the bath,

Wondering just how long I can dwell.

Soaking away in the bath,

Is a favourite pastime of mine,

Drifting away in the moment,

Totally feeling sublime,

Closing my eyes with a sigh,

Just soaking away in the bath,

Then you come in and use the toilet,

You must be having a laugh.

☺

The World's Gone Mad

☺

Health & Safety Gone Mad

Immunity versus Insanity,

That's the world we now live in,

Don't do this and don't do that,

You find you cannot win,

One week to the next,

There's a another pointless scare,

The world has gone health and safety mad,

But I really couldn't care,

Life is for the living,

And I think I can decide,

Whether something's good for me,

And so far I haven't died,

If you gave up all that's described as,

'Being bad for you',

You'd stay at home and starve to death,

By the time you're twenty-two.

Super Sofa Savings Scheme

I used to have a piggy bank,

But it would never fill,

It seemed to have a crack in it,

From which my cash would spill,

I tried to save in my bank account,

But that just didn't work out,

The bills would chomp through all my cash,

And I'd be left with nowt.

But then one day I realised,

When my pockets were mysteriously bare,

The best place to deposit my savings,

Is in the Bank of the Arm Chair,

The Arm Chair Bank is clever,

It has a Sofa Savings Scheme,

It's totally secure and is,

A Super Saver's dream.

You don't have to carry debit cards,

There are no statements or cheques,

There are no hidden bank charges,

And the terms are not complex,

Depositing is really easy,

You just sit on your derrière,

While cash falls from your pocket,

Straight into the Bank of the Arm Chair.

Keep Your Germs to Yourself

You're coughing and sneezing,

I cringe with fear,

"I'm sick" you say while wheezing,

It's that time of year.

I was brought up with manners,

So I want to be polite,

Please cover your mouth,

You inconsiderate little shite.

Did your mother teach you nothing?

No one wants your germs,

Are you five years old?

Will you ever learn?

Don't make me come over there,

And make this into an issue,

Cover your mouth when you cough,

And please sneeze into a tissue.

January Sales Shopping v the OCD Challenged

I'm a tidy Person,

Everything has a place,

But by ten past ten on a Saturday,

I find Primark a disgrace.

TK Max is just as bad,

You can never find what you need,

But when it comes to the January Sales,

I feel very troubled indeed.

Because shopping is hard,

It's a trial at times,

But for the OCD challenged,

It can mess with your mind.

The sizes are higgledy-piggledy,

And the colours are all mixed up,

You want to find some order,

And feel the need to tidy up.

I'd love to find a shop,

Where purchasing is a pleasure,

Where is doesn't take me hours,

And a map to find my treasure.

Train Spotter Extraordinaire

Train spotter extraordinaire,

You'll find him at the station,

It's a pretty regular affair,

That needs no explanation.

Protected by his anorak,

Against the harsh summer sun,

A permanent hunch upon his back,

As he logs his missing one.

His bag contains a flask of tea,

And sandwiches made by his mother,

His one true love is trains you see,

For him there is no other.

Rain or shine he's always there,

Notebook and pen in hand,

A constipated focused stare,

He always gets his man....

Well, train.

Advice for the out-of-Work Teen

Pull up your trousers and go get yourself a job,

I don't pay my taxes for you to act like a slob.

Show some respect, get out there and earn a living,

I'm sick of your attitude of taking and not giving.

The world owes you nothing; let's get one thing straight,

Life's not a talent show; you'll get nothing on a plate.

Stop showing off your boxers, it's time that you got smart,

You can go and get yourself a good haircut for a start.

Get with the real world, life's not a computer game,

You can't mess things up for others to take the blame.

Accept responsibility, grow up and get some balls,

Do yourself a favour and stop driving me up the wall.

Planet You

I'd love to be a resident of the planet you live on,

Where nothing is your fault and you are never wrong,

Where everyone but you has to take the blame,

And in your self-importance you find your own fame.

It seems your ability to listen without butting in,

Is as non-existent as your talent for understanding,

You have no compassion for others you always put yourself first,

And as for having enemies, you are your worst.

You always go on about how your glass is half empty,

When, if you had half as much, it would still be plenty,

And while on 'Planet You' there certainly is no mistaking,

If you aren't the current topic then a change is in the making.

Because every conversation has to be about you,

And the words "Are you OK?" seem to be your cue,

To start a barrage of bemoaning on how your life is such a hardship,

When, really, compared to others it's just an insignificant blip,

People drop subtle hints coz unlike you they are too kind,

But your skin is even thicker than an elephant's hide,

Of course you'll never realise this poem is all about you,

Because you'll never see yourself like other people do.

Queue Jumpers Beware

How could you not notice that bloody great queue?

We're not all sat here just enjoying the view,

You speed down the inside like the cars are not here,

Then you suddenly think "I want to be over there".

You slam on your brakes and put your indicator on,

You act like you're innocent; you've done nothing wrong.

When deep down inside you know exactly what you've done,

You've gone and beaten the queue you son-of-a-gun.

I've been queuing for ages I'm not going to let you in,

Queue Jumper, you annoy me I will not let you win!

I try to ignore you; pretend you're not there,

As you display on your face, a desperate stare.

As acting goes it's a pretty good plea,

But I'm not that stupid did you think I didn't see?

I stare straight ahead avoiding contact with your eyes,

Then you start over-gesturing with shoulder shrugs and whys?

What possessed you to think that I'd let you in,

While your nudging your car wearing a know-it-all grin.

I've not queued all this time to give up my space,

You can wipe that stupid grin right off your face.

You give up and move on to the person in front,

Trying it on again, you annoying little twunt,

"Oh, please don't let him in!" I yell with dismay,

Like the person in front can hear what I say.

They've only gone and done it, they've let him win,

By waving him over and letting him in,

It makes me feel angry right to the core,

That the bloody queue jumper has just won the war,

But this war is not over; you just wait and see,

An elephant never forgets and that elephant is me,

I make a mental picture of his car and his grin,

For the next time Queue Jumper you're not going to win.

Fad Diet Bimbo Part 2 – Faking It at the Gym

She's a Fad Diet Bimbo,

She's faking it at the gym,

How can she have *real* boobs that big,

And still be so bloody slim?

She never bothers running,

Well it's not a big surprise,

Because a light jog on the treadmill,

Could give her two black eyes.

Why does she bother turning up,

In her skimpy gym attire,

Complete with leopard thong leotard,

That can't surely go much higher?

Her face is plastered up with make-up,

Applied with a builder's trowel,

Never breaking into a sweat,

So tell me why she needs that towel?

Her fake nails tap on her mobile,

Clicking out some bimbo code,

About Botox, fake hair and face lifts,

And that new fad diet that's in Vogue.

She sets the machine to easy,

And sits there chatting to her friend,

About how she's going for McDonalds,

As soon as her workout ends.

She's a Fad Diet Bimbo,

She's faking it at the gym,

How can she have real boobs that big,

And still be so bloody slim?

For God's Sake Why the Remake

Turn on, tune in for the movie listed on TV tonight,

A Nightmare on Elm Street but something isn't right?

Hang on just one minute, that's not what I recall,

This movie isn't anything like I remember it at all.

That's not Robert Englund, the 'Freddy Krueger' master,

Oh crikey it's a remake, that's not what I was after.

For God's sake why the remake,

Is there nothing out there that's new?

I'm sick of knowing the ending,

Before joining the cinema queue.

I'm going to boycott your remakes,

It's time to make a stand,

It'll have to be something original,

Before my money leaves my hand.

I turn to the cinema schedule to find out what is on,

Carrie, another remake, there's something rather wrong.

Has no one got the imagination to bring us something new?

A movie that makes us want to pay and join the cinema queue.

A trip for two to the cinema is now just shy of twenty quid,

I may as well just watch the movies I saw when I was a kid.

For God's sake why the remake,

Is there nothing out there that's new?

I'm sick of knowing the ending,

Before joining the cinema queue.

I'm going to boycott your remakes,

It's time to make a stand,

It'll have to be something original,

Before my money leaves my hand.

☺

☺

Horrifying Rhymes

☺

Zombies Don't Run

OI! Movie directors,

Zombies don't run,

They don't have brains,

They can't climb walls,

And they definitely can't use a gun.

OI! Movie directors,

Please keep to the rules,

They can't open doors,

Or walk through walls,

You're confusing them with ghouls.

OI! Movie directors,

Please stick to the script,

They stumble around,

Looking for brains,

After emerging from their crypt.

OI! Movie directors,

This really isn't fun,

It's time you got it,

Into your head,

That ZOMBIES DON'T RUN.

On the Day the Martians Landed (Ode to H G Wells)

On the day the Martians landed,

We thought they'd come in peace,

Naively we tried to make new friends,

Until they killed the priest.

They'd come with just one agenda,

Complete world domination,

And with their heat ray they began,

Total annihilation.

Tri-pedal sphere's that towered over,

The likes of London's Big Ben,

Seemingly immune to all our weapons,

But the flu took care of them.

Stealth Cat

Come back from work and he's there,

Sat still with a scornful fixed stare,

Turn your back on him if you dare,

For Stealth Cat is one moggie to beware.

He's faster than the speed of light,

And as sleek and as dark as the night,

He materialises to give you a fright,

But his meow isn't as bad as his bite.

Stealth Cat's in his Camo-Cat disguise,

The only things visible are his green eyes,

In the shadows like a ninja he hides,

While he schemes on your quick demise.

His claws are as sharp as dress pins,

Exactly what he needs to remove skin,

And before you've noticed he's in,

Your tea has gone and he's out on the bin.

In everyday life you have to take care,

Fear for your life while walking upstairs,

Because Stealth Cat can come from nowhere,

To take you down with no more than a scare.

What You Don't See Scares You More

Horror films are great,

But forget the blood and gore,

Because believe me when I say,

What you don't see scares you more.

What's lurking in that cupboard?

What's hiding under the bed?

Are those demons real?

Or are they're just there in your head?

Are there monsters in the dark?

Are they hiding behind that door?

Now you are starting to believe that,

What you don't see scares you more.

What was that scary noise?

Is there something in your house?

Could it be a poltergeist?

Or is it just a mouse?

As you shiver in your boots,

You realise now for sure,

That the imagination is creepier and,

What you don't see scares you more.

Skeleton Bob

There's a skeleton in my closet,

He says his name is Bob,

He spends his time just hanging around,

Because he hasn't got a job.

Frankenstein and His Monster

When discussing the films of this popular novel,

It's a regular source of confusion,

That the Monster itself is called Frankenstein,

Seems to be the common conclusion.

But I'm here to put you straight,

Frankenstein was not the Monster's name,

Frankenstein was his creator,

And it's the film makers that are to blame.

When you see the poster for the film,

It's always the monster that's shown,

Pictured under the word 'Frankenstein',

And that's how the confusion has grown.

Of course there was Bride of Frankenstein,

Where Frankenstein created a wife,

But the bride was created for the Monster,

Again, adding to all of this strife.

Mary Shelley could be to blame too,

For never giving the Monster a name,

For the Monster could only be judged as so,

Sadly, adding again to this claim.

Although Frankenstein was a monster of a man,

He was not the Monster in question,

And the Monster was not really a monster,

He just couldn't handle his aggression.

Clowns

Whoever said clowns are funny,

Must have been having a laugh,

Because a person who hides,

Behind a greasepaint mask,

Couldn't be any scarier by half.

Their face is painted up to be happy,

Hiding their true expression,

When deep down inside,

A killer could hide,

By giving off a false impression.

Writer's Revenge

You'd better watch yourself,
I'm coming after to you,
You best stay on my good side,
There's no telling what I'll do.

Forget bog-standard murder,
It's been done time and again,
My revenge is sweeter,
Because I'll do it with my pen.

I'll write you as a victim,
Of a very brutal killer,
Who'll bury you in bananas,
And feed you to a gorilla.

Or maybe something worse,
I'll pen you a slow death,
Sat on by an elephant,
Until you've breathed your last breath.

How about death by drowning,
"Well that's not so strange" you say,
But in a vat of custard,
You don't see that every day.

Or nibbled to death by squirrels,
Addicted to peanut butter,
Applied thickly with a toothbrush,
By a squirrel-loving nutter.

It could be death by tickling,

With pink and purple feathers,

By a maniac with a fetish,

Dressed head to toe in leathers.

There's so many different ways,

I can kill you with my pen,

And if I change my mind on how,

I can just go do it again.

Mummies v Zombies

Isn't a mummy just a zombie when it rises from its tomb?

Or is it classified as different because it has its own room?

Whether a mummy or a zombie they adopt the same pose,

It seems the only difference is what they wear for clothes.

A zombie is more dapper because it has its mourning suit,

Whereas a mummy is wrapped in bandages head to boot.

They both stagger around like they are on a pub crawl,

I wonder who would win if the two of them were to brawl?

Fly-By Teleportation

I'm going to start a company called Fly-By Teleportation,

It's going to be the greatest innovation in transportation.

No longer will you have to be stuck in traffic queues,

You can go to anyplace you want anytime you choose.

Never again will you feel the need to drive your car,

Or board an aeroplane if you want to travel far.

Just jump in our machine and choose your destination,

Press the big green button and you'll be there, no hesitation.

The machine is only built for one so make sure it's just you,

As we cannot be held responsible if you teleport with two.

Of course with this kind of travel you may feel some side effects,

But we'll do our best to provide you with the necessary checks.

If you feel a little unsettled or start to crave something that's sweet,

Or feel the need to puke on your food before you start to eat.

Please contact our customer service team and quote the word 'Fly',

We guarantee we'll send our best extermination team by.

☺

Shits & Giggles

☺

Act like a Lady

My dad always said, "Act like a lady",

And I always did my best,

But I could never hide my talents,

So I'd burp and fart with the rest.

I learnt how to burp while saying 'Pardon',

So it wouldn't seem quite so rude,

But I had to be very careful,

Not to regurgitate my food.

You can insist on me wearing dresses,

But that will never disguise the fact,

That I cannot act like a lady,

Maybe it's time you accepted that.

Toilet SOS

As I reached for the paper my eye shed a tear,

Grasping at thin air I realised my worst fear,

I'd sat on the throne and forgotten to check,

Was the public toilet completely to spec?

How could I have forgotten the first rule of thumb?

To sit there unaware as I emptied my bum,

The embarrassment I faced was too much to bear,

But as it dried to my butt I just couldn't sit here.

I called from my stall 'Is there anyone there?'

From the tone of my voice you could hear my despair,

Silence followed my echo I was all on my own,

Do I leave the stall or do I reach for my phone?

A simple case of gender discrimination,

Meant sadly a phone call was out of the question,

I knew I was in trouble the shit had truly hit the pan,

The only person close enough to call was a man.

With my handbag round my neck and clothes gathered with care,

I shuffled to the next stall with my arse completely bare,

Should anyone enter they would think me a loon,

As they were awkwardly exposed to my dirty full moon.

Thank heavens I'd made it before someone came in,

But as I sat on the seat a new fear crept in,

What if all the stalls were the same as the last?

Devoid of the paper designed to clean arse.

I sighed with relief as I reached for the roll,

And found there was paper to clean up my hole,

The moral of this story is to be better prepared,

Keep tissue in your bag so embarrassment is spared.

Spot Picker

As I look into the mirror,

'Mount Whitehead' rears its head,

My fingers start their twitching,

And my heart is filled with dread.

I know if I start squeezing,

That the whiteheads will just spread,

And that a single pus-filled spot,

Becomes a mountain range instead.

I just can't help myself,

I've just got to see that goo,

I can't explain the satisfaction,

It's just something that I do,

You'd think I was a teen,

But I've just turned forty-two,

With a face that's just like a pizza,

There's only one thing I can do.

I cannot help but squeeze it,

I've tried all of the creams,

I try just to ignore it,

But inside a voice just screams,

'Come on Spot Picker, squeeze it,

It's the whitehead of your dreams.',

As I push each side the pressure builds,

And the top begins to gleam.

It's like I've conquered Everest,

The joy upon the release,

First the pain and then the gain,

As the mirror's smeared with grease,

I feel a warm contentment,

My mind should be at peace,

But it isn't really over yet,

I'm an addict who won't cease.

There's still a massive lump,

There must be a second store,

And as I squeeze again it weeps,

And it starts feeling a bit sore,

Just one more squeeze I say,

Then the blood begins to pour,

So I leave it for an hour,

Then try again to find some more.

By the time that I am finished,

There's still an angry lump,

It's redder than anything ever seen,

And now I've got the hump,

I just can't leave it alone,

Despite the throbbing thump,

There's got to be more in there,

So I get the suction pump.

Now here I am in hospital,

Having surgery on my face,

To fill the giant crater that,

Should only belong in space,

To prevent me making it worse,

They've got me tied in place,

And I won't be seeing home soon,

Coz they've judged me a nut-case.

The Wee That Just Won't Wait

You find you cannot stand up straight,

With the wee that just won't wait,

You turn a wiggle into a dance,

While holding on is a game of chance.

But there's no time to contemplate,

With the wee that just won't wait,

You change position and cross your legs,

But the call of nature it still begs.

You find you just can't concentrate,

With the wee that just won't wait,

You need a convenient place to stop,

But it's caught you on the hop.

You're now in a desperate state,

With the wee that just won't wait,

And you find it's all gone wrong,

Because you've left it far too long.

You realise that you really hate,

That wee that just won't wait,

And you will never ever forget,

Now your trousers are all wet.

Shits & Giggles

It's all shits and giggles,

Until someone giggles and shits,

It's the very worst in oops moments,

That can make us feel like proper twits.

Curry Poo

NB: This is written to the tune of Chim Chim Cher-ee from the film Mary Poppins

Ring Sting-ery Ring Sting-ery good gracious me,

It's coming from my butt with the texture of wee,

Ring Sting-ery Ring Sting-ery its curry poo,

There's nowt like a curry that comes back to haunt you.

As I sit on the toilet I know I've been stung,

That curry I enjoyed won't only burn my tongue,

As it revisits this world it is really no joke,

With a stench that makes my eyes water oh how I do choke.

Ring Sting-ery Ring Sting-ery good gracious me,

It's coming from my butt with the texture of wee,

Ring Sting-ery Ring Sting-ery its curry poo,

There's nowt like a curry that comes back to haunt you.

Ring Sting-ery Ring Sting-ery good gracious me,

It's coming from my butt with the texture of wee,

Ring Sting-ery Ring Sting-ery its curry poo,

There's nowt like a curry that comes back to haunt you.

The pressure is on you can feel it pushing through,

There's no holding back when you need a curry poo,

You sit on the toilet and release the world,

Then wish for a gas mask as the stench is unfurled.

Who'd have thought when I was eating that curry last night,

That the meal would return with the early morning light,

But from the noises I'm making this is really not right,

And as I bite down on the door handle I try not to fight.

Ring Sting-ery Ring Sting-ery good gracious me,

It's coming from my butt with the texture of wee,

Ring Sting-ery Ring Sting-ery its curry poo,

There's nowt like a curry that comes back to haunt you.

Ifs, Butts & Impressionists

I appear to have an impressionist,

Who resides inside my butt,

He can toot just like a train,

And quack just like a duck,

Whenever it's a foggy day,

He sounds off a good fog horn,

And he makes a great alarm clock,

Because he tends to wake up at dawn.

Clean Up Your Poo

Clean up your dog shit and your horse shit too,

No one wants to walk through your animal's poo,

No one wants to take the quick brown slide,

Through the steaming great pile your horse left behind.

A couple take a romantic walk through the park,

Eyes focused on each other as the day grows dark,

Not looking where they are going as the sun begins to set,

When, oops, the date is over coz you didn't clean behind your pet.

Clean up your dog shit and your horse shit too,

No one wants to walk through your animal's poo,

No one wants to take the quick brown slide,

Through the steaming great pile your horse left behind.

Mum has been cleaning and she's really house-proud,

When the kids come home with friends it's a really large crowd,

They scramble through living room to see what's on TV,

Their shoes tracking stains from the poo they didn't see.

Clean up your dog shit and your horse shit too,

No one wants to walk through your animal's poo,

No one wants to take the quick brown slide,

Through the steaming great pile your horse left behind.

It's very easy to do just Google 'horse nappy',

Buy this neat invention to stop our paths from getting crappy.

To stop the little disasters involving your dog's shit,

On walks master the talent of how to bag and bin it.

Clean up your dog shit and your horse shit too,

No one wants to walk through your animal's poo,

No one wants to take the quick brown slide,

Through the steaming great pile your horse left behind.

The Festival's Festering Toilets

The trouble with festival toilets,

Is I really just can't seem to go,

It doesn't matter how desperate I am,

Nothing will help with the flow.

I've worked out the best time to visit,

Is just after the cleaners have been,

But you're really up shit-creek with no paddle,

When you wake up to find you've lain in.

The best thing to do is start queuing,

As the cleaners are working their magic,

That way you can guarantee a nice clean seat,

And not sitting on something that's tragic.

But sometimes nature calls at night,

And there's really no way to hold on,

And the next part of my poem describes,

The challenge that you're put upon.

Visualise, if you can,

The power to hold on is long gone,

You struggle into your clothes and boots,

And navigate your way with torch on.

You walk on with trepidation,

Unsure of just what you might find,

You pray that you'll find a clean toilet,

On which to sit your behind.

You are met with a horrible stink,

As you open the Port-a-Loo door,

You try to keep yourself from being sick,

Until the torchlight shows what's on the floor.

How the hell did it get into this state?

For God's sake where the hell is the cleaner?

As you are met with a big pile of excrement,

And a smell that couldn't make you much greener.

When it comes to the festival toilets,

There's a certain amount of disobedience,

To leaving them as you'd like to find them,

They are an underappreciated convenience.

Why is it Always Carrots?

Whether a night out on the town,

Or that bug that's going around,

Why is it whenever I am sick,

There are always carrots in it?

A dodgy chicken delight,

With not a single carrot in sight,

But when my stomach decides to erupt,

It's always carrots I seem to bring up.

It doesn't matter if I don't eat at all,

And spend the night by the toilet bowl,

Whenever I'm sick as a parrot,

Why is it always carrots?

☺

On A More Serious Note

☺

Two Wrongs Won't Make It Right

An eye for an eye,

A tooth for a tooth,

Do we really need to kill,

To discover the truth?

So the saying goes,

'Revenge is sweet',

And while the World's like this,

Peace cannot compete.

We all dream of a world,

Where harmony reigns,

Where, differences aside,

Acceptance remains,

But while each side fights,

And neither feels contrite,

How many times must we say,

TWO WRONGS WON'T MAKE IT RIGHT.

The Comedian's Grin

I fake a smile,

When all the while,

My world is upside down,

With every sigh,

And 'happy' lie,

I conceal my saddest frown,

I tell my jokes,

To the laughing blokes,

Who see me as a clown,

But once I'm home,

I feel so alone,

That my sorrow's I must drown.

Busker's Blues

Standing on the pavement,

Outside the shopping centre,

The busker plays his heart out,

Despite the chilling weather,

Strumming on his one possession,

A worn out acoustic guitar,

Familiar songs he's learnt by ear,

Knowing he'll never go far,

An old margarine tub is laid out,

Collecting for his next meal,

But the shoppers trundle past him,

Pretending he's not real,

Or maybe they just don't hear him,

Because they're permanently plugged in,

To their hundred pound iPod's,

While throwing half a pasty in the bin,

The busker sings the blues,

A song about worries and troubles,

As shoppers happily walk on by,

While his empty stomach rumbles.

Mobile Distractions

Is that something in your pocket?

Or are you just pleased to see me?

Oh, it's your mobile,

Why can't you just leave it be?

It's a conversation killer,

Every time you get it out,

Just leave it alone for five minutes,

We'd have more to talk about.

Whether it's a text conversation,

When you're driving home from work,

Or a quick update on Facebook,

That makes you drive like a berk,

You're oblivious to the fact,

That you're breaking the law,

Or will it take a fatal accident,

Before you realise the score?

Mobiles drive me to distraction,

When they're distracting you from life,

Whether it takes you away from your task,

Or a polite conversation with your wife,

Before you destroy something precious,

Put down your mobile phone,

Pay more attention to what you're doing,

Declare it a Mobile Free Zone.

Bright Sparks

When winter comes round it's a win,

For the energy firms who aren't dim,

As the weather gets colder,

Their nerves becomes bolder,

And we all have to take it on the chin.

As we put up our celebratory lights,

Their prices go up to new heights,

Merry Christmas they say,

But your pocket will pay,

For displaying your seasonal delights.

As the temperature goes down to zero,

And the need for some heating does grow,

Forgotten are the old,

Choosing to eat or be cold,

While energy firms pretend they don't know.

Death of a Bulwell Badger

I saw a dead badger today,

He must have come a long way,

To be quite near the centre of town,

Laying there dead on the ground.

Maybe he was heading for the shops,

To pick up a couple of chops,

Or maybe he was looking for a new home,

Because where he used to live, houses had grown.

It was sad to see him lying there,

Clearly hit by a driver who didn't care,

Having avoided Britain's badger cull,

That helps keep them under control.

The next day I saw a dead fox,

Just up the road from Badger's sad corpse,

He'd been munching on squirrel road kill,

When he met with a car radiator grill.

The day after I saw a dead rabbit,

Who had crossed a new road out of habit,

It had been fields when she'd last gone that way,

Until the town's bypass was finished today.

Then poor squirrel, a species that mates for life,

Witnessed the death of his poor squirrel wife,

I can guess but didn't see what had happened,

But he was dragging her body that was flattened.

The animals were dropping like flies,

So I looked into the cause of their demise,

It chilled me right to the bone,

To realise their homes were all gone.

They'd been driven away to make space,

For the ever-growing human race,

Who were continuing to take over Planet Earth,

Without considering just how much it was worth.

Now I am sorry this is a sad tale of woe,

But this really seemed the only way to show,

Of how we ignore all of the animal's pleas,

And turn away and just do what we please.

How would we like it if we went home one day,

To find our lives and homes destroyed in this way,

To come back and find everything gone,

Because someone didn't think it was wrong.

Don't Believe a Bully

You're a special individual,

No matter what they say,

You're beautiful the way you are,

Don't let them stand in your way.

Don't believe a bully,

Keep both feet on the ground,

Because growing up is hard enough,

Without bullies to bring you down.

To make themselves feel better,

They need to pick on you,

It's best to just ignore them,

Don't let them get to you.

Don't believe a bully,

Believe in yourself,

You're the one that matters,

You don't need their kind of help.

A bully's opinion,

Doesn't count for much

It built from insecurity,

And a personal lack of trust.

Don't believe a bully,

Don't let them make you blue,

Don't let their lies destroy your life,

Because the world is better with you.

Ghost Town Shopping

Child of the future speaking to her Grandparent:

Do you remember what it was like when the high street had so many shops?

When you'd walk around window shopping or pop in to buy some chops.

Do you remember the town before estate agents and pub chains took over?

When you used to go in for the day to buy shoes and maybe a pullover?

Does anyone know what happened to make the high street so run-down?

Did it coincide with online shopping? Did that make the shops all close down?

Grandparent describing the past:

I remember a time of record shops, book shops and clothes shops galore,

A time when I loved shopping and left wanting more,

A time when you took a day out just to go into town,

To buy what you wanted or just to look around,

A time before computers brought us 'buy with one click',

A time when a shopping trip would never be quick.

Grandparent explaining why:

It's sad that we never supported our high street,

Never used the butchers to buy our fresh meat,

Forgotten were the greengrocers and bakers alike,

Now they're not there we miss them alright.

This is an insight into what the future may hold,

If we don't support the high street, now you've been told.

Don't Judge a Banana by Its Skin

Don't judge a banana by its skin,

Because it doesn't determine what's within.

Don't use a movie to judge a book,

And you should never judge someone by just a look.

A chilli might not be as hot once you've tried,

And the Tardis is not so small on the inside,

Give someone a chance before you form your opinion,

And don't let life dictate to you like you are its minion.

Christmas Cheer

It's the first week in December and Christmas draws near,

I've never really looked forward to this time of year.

Shopping centres clog up with people driven by greed,

Spending far too much money on stuff they don't need.

Some spend more than they have and then sink into debt,

Have their kids really got to have everything they can get?

Like that Xbox game which costs the equivalent of a day's wages,

How did we get this bad as we progressed through the ages?

It is worse in the supermarket as gluttony comes out,

Because piling up our trollies is what Christmas is all about!

Legs bow on the tables laden with a Christmas Dinner,

With three kinds of meat it will surely be a winner.

Enough sides and desserts that you could feed a whole town,

While somewhere in the world there's not enough to go round.

Then comes the aftermath as bins overflow,

With paper and cards and food spoils that must go.

We're a nation of wasters that really cannot see,

What Christmas is about, how it really should be.

An Austerity Christmas is what our house is having,

With a small present each covered in recycled wrapping.

We're only going to buy what we know we can eat,

With a few special biscuits and wine for a treat.

To you this may sound boring but we do it every year,

And it doesn't stop us from having our Christmas Cheer.

☺

☺

CREDITS

My influences for writing these poems.

☺

Starring:

Duvet Deadlock – Influenced by wanting to stay in bed in the morning.

What *not* to Do While in Your Own World – Influenced by observational traffic jams.

Everyone Has an Alter Ego except for Me – Influenced by my longing to be a superhero and save the world.

Star Wars the Movie Soap Opera – Influenced by my love of Star Wars.

Transfer Window Blues – Influenced by my frustrations every transfer window time.

I Blame You Barbara Cartland – Influenced by the lying romance novels I used to read while at school.

Mind Your P'S & Q's – Influenced by the lack of manners people seem to have now-a-days.

MISSING! One Sock – Influenced by lost socks and love.

Holiday Sickness – Influenced by the amount of times I've become ill while on my holidays.

Devils DIY – Influenced by how rubbish I am at painting gloss on wood.

Me & My Yellow Car – Influenced by my yellow car and the yellow car game.

Remote Access – Influenced by my ongoing to struggle to win the TV remote.

My Brother & I – Influenced by my childhood with my lovely brother.

All It Take Is Just a Smile – Influenced by the friendly chap down my street who waves, smiles and brightens my mornings.

Granddad Groaners – Influenced by my wonderful granddad's sense of humour. RIP Granddad Jim.

Money Tree – Influenced by my lucky money tree.

Sorry I Nearly Forgot – Influenced by how forgetful I am sometimes.

I Am Who I Am – Influenced by me being myself and not what others think I should be.

Ode to My Best Friend – Written for my best friend.

Soaking Away in the Bath – Influenced by my ongoing struggle to have a nice relaxing bath without someone wanting the toilet.

☺

Co-Starring:

Health & Safety Gone Mad – Influenced by our bubble-wrapped, common-senseless society.

Super Sofa Savings Scheme – Influenced by how poor saving schemes are now-a-days.

Keep Your Germs to Yourself – My on-going fight to stop people sharing their germs.

January Sale Shopping V the OCD Challenged – Influenced by how much I hate shopping in disorganised stores.

Train Spotter Extraordinaire – About the average train spotter.

Advice for the out-of-Work Teen – For the teenagers who think they can sit on their butt all day and do nothing.

Planet You – About that self-absorbed person who can do nothing more than make everything about them.

Queue Jumpers Beware – Influenced by my annoyance at people who think they don't have to queue.

Fad Diet Bimbo Part 2 ~ Faking It at the Gym – Influenced by the skinny bimbo who complains that she is fat.

For God's Sake Why the Remake – Influenced by my annoyance that the film industry can't come up with anything new now-a-days.

Zombies Don't Run – Influenced by the movie World War Z.

On the Day the Martians Landed (Ode to H G Wells) – Influenced by one of my favourite books, The War of The Worlds.

Stealth Cat – Influenced by my mum's last cat Bertie. RIP Bert.

What You Don't See Scares You More – Influenced by how spooky it is to not see something in a horror film.

Skeleton Bob – Influenced by the Winter Olympics.

Frankenstein and His Monster – Trying to put straight the confusion that hangs around Frankenstein.

Clowns – Because they're scary!

Writers Revenge – Because sometimes people make you want to.

Mummies v Zombies – Influenced by the question of who would win this fight.

Fly-By Teleportation – Influenced by my want to be able to teleport rather than drive.

☺

With Special Appearance From:

Act Like a Lady – Influenced by the pressure girls are under to behave 'properly'.

Toilet SOS – Influenced by the trouble you can get in when your find yourself without toilet paper.

Spot Picker – About how I just can't leave a whitehead alone.

The Wee That Just Won't Wait – Hold on a minute....No, sorry, I couldn't.

Shits & Giggles – A little ditty about giggling too much.

Curry Poo – Influenced by the day after the Work's Xmas Do Curry Night. Written to the tune of 'Chim Chim Cher-ee' from the film Mary Poppins

Ifs, Butts & Impressionists – Influenced by funny sounding farts.

Clean up Your Poo – Influenced by how some dog and horse owners just leave their animals poo lying around.

The Festivals Festering Toilets – Advice for using festival toilets.

Why is it Always Carrots? – It's a good question, where do the carrots come from?

Two Wrong Won't Make It Right – Influenced by the sad death of Drummer Lee Rigby.

The Comedian's Grin – Influenced by how someone can look one way on the outside but feel completely different on the inside.

Busker's Blues – Influenced by the hungry buskers of the world.

Mobile Distractions – Influenced by how many people I see using their phone while driving.

Bright Sparks – Influenced by the ever increasing energy bills.

The Death of a Bulwell Badger – Written after seeing a dead badger on the side of the road in town.

Don't Believe a Bully – Influenced by the increasing suicides of victims of bullying.

Ghost Town Shopping – Influenced by the decreasing shops in towns due to online shopping.

Don't Judge a Banana by Its Skin – Influenced by dislike racism.

Christmas Cheer – Influenced by the amount of money we spend on Christmas when we can't afford it.

☺

www.ingramcontent.com/pod-product-compliance
Lightning Source LLC
Chambersburg PA
CBHW060948040426
42445CB00011B/1060